CONTE

CHOIC

Will Harris • *RENDANG* • Granta Poetry

RECOMMENDATIONS

Claire Crowther • *Solar Cruise* • Shearsman
Carolyn Forché • *In The Lateness of the World* • Bloodaxe
Danez Smith • *Homie* • Chatto
Marvin Thompson • *Road Trip* • Peepal Tree Press

SPECIAL COMMENDATION

Srinivas Rayaprol • *Angular Desire: Selected Poems and Prose* • Carcanet

RECOMMENDED TRANSLATION

Christel Wiinblad • *My Little Brother* • Valley Press
Translated by Marlene Engelund

PAMPHLET CHOICE

Síofra McSherry • *Requiem* • The Emma Press

WILD CARD

Jennifer Wong • *Letters Home* • Nine Arches Press

REVIEWS
LISTINGS

Poetry Book Society

CHOICE SELECTORS RECOMMENDATION SPECIAL COMMENDATION	SANDEEP PARMAR & VIDYAN RAVINTHIRAN
TRANSLATION SELECTOR	GEORGE SZIRTES
PAMPHLET SELECTORS	A.B. JACKSON & DEGNA STONE
WILD CARD SELECTOR	ANTHONY ANAXAGOROU
CONTRIBUTORS	SOPHIE O'NEILL NATHANIEL SPAIN
EDITORIAL & DESIGN	ALICE KATE MULLEN

Membership Options

Magazine Only 4 *Bulletins* a year (UK £22, Europe £35, Rest of the World £42)
Choice 4 Choice books and 4 *Bulletins* a year (£55, £65, £75) **Students** (£35, £55, £65)
Translation Only 4 Translation books and 4 *Bulletins* (£65, £90, £99)
World Poetry 4 Choices, 4 Translation books and 4 *Bulletins* (£98, £120, £132)
Charter 20 Choices and Recommendations and 4 *Bulletins* (£180, £210, £235)
Complete 24 Choices, Recommendations, Translations and 4 *Bulletins* (£223, £265, £292)
School Basic 4 books, 4 *Bulletins*, posters, teaching notes (£79, £89, £99)
School Advanced 20 books, 4 *Bulletins*, posters, teaching notes (£209, £245, £275)
Single copies of the *Bulletin* £9.99

Cover Art Laboni Islam - Poet, artist and PBS Member

Poetry Book Society | Milburn House | Dean Street | Newcastle upon Tyne | NE1 1LF
0191 230 8100 | enquiries@poetrybooksociety.co.uk
WWW.POETRYBOOKS.CO.UK

LETTER FROM THE PBS

How to introduce the brilliant selections this season? I have struggled to find the right words for this short letter. Broadly, they contain reflections and responses to the death of loved ones, notions of home and belonging, they delve into the complexity of speech, poetry and language. And the books themselves are little objects of art.

The poet commentaries in this Spring *Bulletin* are brilliant, they add moving and thoughtful context which will really enhance your reading of their collections. I hope the selectors' and poets' pieces inspire you, as much as they have the team at PBS, to pick up these brilliant collections and read and reflect.

It is with sadness that we say farewell to our current selectors Vidyan Ravinthiran, George Szirtes, A.B. Jackson and Degna Stone. I'd like to take this opportunity to say a huge thank you to each of them for their commitment to finding the absolute best the season has to offer and for their insightful commentaries. We will miss you all. We'd also like to extend a warm welcome to our new selectors Sinéad Morrissey, Andrew McMillan, Nick Makoha, Mary Jean Chan and Ilya Kaminsky. We look forward forward to sharing their selections with you later this year.

We have our first public event of 2020 taking place in Edinburgh on 3rd April at the wonderful Scottish Poetry Library, featuring Denise Riley, Charlotte Ansell and Juana Adcock – please keep an eye on our website and newsletter for details.

We are delighted to announce the winners of the 2019 PBS & Mslexia Women's Poetry Competition. Judge Malika Booker claimed: "The poems submitted were brave, experimental, found poems, traditional, formal and challenging in both theme, and subject matter." Many thanks to all who entered and congratulations to the prize winners and their poems: Regi Claire, '(Un) certainties'; Jacqueline Saphra, 'Fishwife'; Alex Toms, 'Daedelus in Therapy'; and Erin Coppin, 'Kindling'. These, and the longlisted poems, can all be read on our website www.poetrybooks.co.uk.

SOPHIE O'NEILL
PBS & INPRESS DIRECTOR

WILL HARRIS

Will Harris is a poet and critic from London. He was shortlisted for the 2018 Forward Prize for Best Single Poem and won a Poetry Fellowship from the Arts Foundation in 2019. He is the author of the chapbook *All This Is Implied* and the essay *Mixed-Race Superman*, published by Peninsula Press in the UK and Melville House in the US. His poems have appeared in *The Guardian, Granta, London Review of Books*, and the anthology *Ten: Poets of the New Generation*. He is co-editing the Spring issue of *The Poetry Review* with Mary Jean Chan.

RENDANG

GRANTA POETRY | £10.99 | PBS PRICE £8.25

Will Harris

Granta Poetry

"A *poem* should not mean / but be," wrote Archibald MacLeish, and I wish he hadn't. Of course poems have a, or many, meanings – they speak of the historical world:

> One day, a white rabbit read
> my fortune, twitching as it chose
>
> from several slips of paper, soft head
> straining at its harness, nose
>
> scabbed, peeled back like bark.
> Here, amid the desert, stark
>
> as day, they tortured dissidents;
> now paper slips blow between
>
> the points of a barbed wire fence.
> A life should not just be, but mean.

'Diyarbakir' – named for the conflict-riven Turkish city – provides one of several wry nods to the canon, and differentiatings from it, in Will Harris's excellent debut. "Here lies one / whose name was writ in *bahasa*" parodies Keats with a cunning truism, because it's the Indonesian, Sanskrit-derived, term for language itself. Poetry so tenderly and contumaciously attentive to the lives of others makes MacLeish – "For all the history of grief / An empty doorway and a maple leaf"– and much contemporary verse – sound facile in comparison:

> Yathu says he went by Church St to find a gift for Mother's Day. He went into five shops and couldn't find a single non-white person, or anything his mum would like. *It was all so dainty.*
>   I tell him that recently strangers have been coming up to me on the street. Yesterday, for example, a man in Shepherd's Bush asked me about the fire.
>
> ME: The fire?
> HIM: Yes. Is it near?
> ME: [silence] Grenfell?
> HIM: Yes!
> ME: I don't know. Fifteen minutes?

Is there a name for the shape of that startling second sentence? I think of zeugma, aligning two unlike things – "the lightning bolt parted him from his life and his chariot", for instance – but the pause dividing the non-finding of "a single non-white person" from the non-finding of anything Yathu's Sri Lankan mum would like, is something else. There's a lot of thinking behind that comma.

WILL HARRIS

Veronica Forrest-Thomson's *Poetic Artifice* introduced me to something Wittgenstein wrote: "Do not forget that a poem, even though it is composed in the language of information, is not used in the language-game of giving information." In his notebook, Wittgenstein prefaces this with a short sentence: "The way music speaks."

But music doesn't speak, or not in sentences. To hear what a poem's saying I sometimes block out all the words except the pronouns, prepositions and conjunctions: *in, they, with, you, here, I.* William James argues that these little words – like musical notes – express some larger "shading or other of relation". They're what constitute the self in its relation to others.

Another thing: Wittgenstein says "not used". He describes what a poem does in the negative. I think one of poetry's main gestures is that of refusal. Every day, as I get dressed or eat a sandwich or talk to friends, I affirm something. Poetry is language *not* used in the service of giving information. It offers a space for refusal; it says no, no, no. This kind of freedom – this potential for freedom – can change us if we let it.

Frantz Fanon writes: "Was my freedom not given to me then in order to build the world of the *You*?" How do we as poets build the world of the You? A lot of the poems I care about start with this question. They do things with the little words – *I, you, we* – that bind us. From them come hope, solidarity, and the strength for refusal.

WILL RECOMMENDS

Recently, like many, I've been turning to the work of the late Sean Bonney: "call it cleanliness call it kindness // do not call it kindness to me // your nobility your spirit / keep it far from me." I've also been altered and inspired by M. NourbeSe Philip's *She Tries Her Tongue, Her Silence Softly Breaks* (1988), and Nathaniel Mackey's newly reissued first book *Eroding Witness* (1985). I've loved beautiful new pamphlets by Jay G. Ying and Jennifer Wong put out by Nina Mingya Powles's *Bitter Melon* 苦瓜. And I think everyone should read Gertrude Stein, Martin Carter and Vahni Capildeo. I've also – I don't know if it helps – been obsessively combing through edickinson.org for grains of resistance: "Till His best step approaching / We journey to the Day / And tell each other how We sung / To keep the Dark away" (F955).

IN WEST SUMATRA

In West Sumatra they call rendang
  randang. Neither shares a root

with rending. Rose and rose
  have French and Frisian roots

you can't hear. Context makes
  the difference clear. Here lies one

whose name was writ in *bahasa*.
  Here are words I've said

in memory of her who I could
  never speak to. Tjandra Sari,

I call you wrongly. Rend me
  rightly. Rootless and unclear.

LINES OF FLIGHT
LONDON

A shuttle flies between
the seasons, smoothest
from spring to summer

when I think of my Chinese
forebears forced to work
a loom. Who'd be alone

today? Migratory birds are
weaving new patterns
in the air, shuttles flying

back and forth. Here. No,
there. I've been missing you.

Image: Caroline Forbes

CLAIRE CROWTHER

Claire Crowther's poems and reviews have appeared in journals including *London Review of Books, Long Poem, New Statesman, P.N. Review, Poetry Review, Poetry Wales, Shearsman* and *The Times Literary Supplement*. Her poems have been widely anthologised including in *The Best British Poetry 2013* (Salt) and *The Best British Poetry 2015* (Salt). She has published three pamphlets and three full collections and was shortlisted for the Aldeburgh Best First Collection prize. Claire was poet in residence at the Royal Mint Museum during 2014-15. The resulting pamphlet *Bare George* was published in 2016. Claire is co-editor of *The Long Poem Magazine*.

SOLAR CRUISE

SHEARSMAN | £9.95 | PBS   PRICE   £7.47

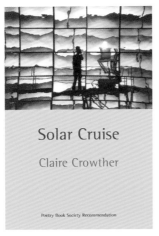

Claire Crowther mosaics together poetic and scientific discourse to create new adventures in thought. Both the poet and the physicist are on a mission of discovery:

> To find which particle is which.
> To hunt the Higgs boson through beam-born bits,
> as many people as live in North America.
>> *It's so shortlived, it's never been*
>> *seen live.*
>
> To saddle sunlight,
>
> to smack the flanks of photons and send up
> data to where a thousand computers stare
> down through their sweating floor to the pantheon.
>
> To name what's been particularised.
>> *Why, how light a thing a boson can be:*
>> *a weightless waving string of photons,*
>> *that hit our retinas, wake us*
>> *to the multiplicity we call nothing.*

These poems perpetually test the ability of science-language to infiltrate the lyric, to begin to make another kind of sense to that which hard science requires. The achievement is never taken for granted. Scientists aren't, as they were in the nineteenth-century, amateurs speaking and writing a language widely understood. Their parlance is necessarily esoteric: you and I might not understand a paper in *Nature*; and that's where popular science comes in, but at the risk of reductiveness, and sensational clickbait which exaggerates what are typically provisional discoveries. There's a problem here – a gap in public understanding – and in that void, Crowther's poems dance and glow:

> Irony 2: The History of the Waist by Lisa Meitner Who Famously
>> Described the Splitting Atom as Waisted
>
>> A man does not have a waist.
>> He has a midriff. A middle.
>> He also has a belly and a breadbasket,
>> a paunch, pot and general girth.
>> A woman has a waist.
>> A woman has been required to identify her waist.
>> A woman gains a neutron to do this.
>> A man remains a spherical uranium nucleus.

Crowther's poems are fizzily cerebral, wordplay-avid, both sensuous and ratiocinative. "I write crosswise. I experiment with words."

CLAIRE CROWTHER

Living with an experimental physicist is a permanent poet's residency in the lab. *Solar Cruise* was inspired by the many conversations I have had with my partner, Keith Barnham (a physicist researching solar energy), about poetry and its ability to name and thus to begin to define the explorations of science. I wanted to record the effort we all make to change the world in words. Keith and I are concerned with how we receive each other in language; talking together is one way to give the self we choose to give and be taken for the self that another person wants to receive.

While it is a love story between a poet and a physicist, it is also a narrative about a scientist willing to say publicly what difference solar electricity could make to the reduction of carbon emission, willing to prophesy to an unfriendly establishment. Language choices have political as well as emotional consequences so conversation about climate change was central to the development of *Solar Cruise*, just as such conversation plays a huge part in developing relevant policies and practices. When I needed to quote him or simply imagine what the character in these poems would say – in *Solar Cruise* Keith became a character I could manipulate imaginatively and I did – then I often wrote his words in his language.

Poetry and science can speak together. The boat that hosts the narrative of *Solar Cruise* is possibly an ark to the new world, possibly a funeral ship from the old world:

> The ship of our time is no tree
> with a yard arm, a mast. No walnut shell rocks us home.
>
> Planes charge across skies, leaves blowing
> away from the branch. But we two travel water-earthed...

CLAIRE RECOMMENDS

Vahni Capildeo, *Skin Can Hold* (Carcanet); Tsvetanka Elenkova, *Crookedness* (Shearsman); Carrie Etter, *The Weather in Normal* (Seren); Geoffrey Hill, *The Book of Baruch by the Gnostic Justin* (OUP); Selima Hill, *I May Be Stupid But I'm Not That Stupid* (Bloodaxe); Martha Kapos, *Smile Variations* (Happenstance); D.S. Marriott, *Duppies* (A.K. Press); Alice Oswald, *Nobody* (Cape); Frances Presley Ada, *Unseen* (Shearsman) and Tamar Yoseloff, *The Black Place* (Seren).

Darkness turns toward   the sun

MARRIAGE, A SUNBEAT

Don't we feel the natural sound of sun
        beating inside itself as any human body beats?

Don't our atoms measure disruption
        into unexpected lines or graphs as we float on?

Do we take ourselves to heart
        and resonate?

Are we all Antarctic ice sheets cracking
        in weakening heat, singing under strain?

Surely the sun gives us our physic.

CLAIRE CROWTHER

CAROLYN FORCHÉ

Carolyn Forché's first volume of poetry, *Gathering the Tribes*, winner of the Yale Series of Younger Poets Prize, was followed by *The Country Between Us*, *The Angel of History*, and *Blue Hour*. She is also the author of the memoir *What You Have Heard Is True* (Penguin Press, 2019), a finalist for the National Book Award and long-listed for the Carnegie Medal. She has translated Mahmoud Darwish, Claribel Alegría, and Robert Desnos. Her famed international anthology, *Against Forgetting*, was praised by Nelson Mandela as "a blow against tyranny, against prejudice, against injustice," and followed by the 2014 anthology *The Poetry of Witness*. In 1998 in Stockholm, she received the Edita and Ira Morris Hiroshima Foundation for Peace and Culture Award for her human rights advocacy and the preservation of memory and culture. She is one of the first poets to receive the Wyndham Campbell Prize, and is a visiting Professor at Newcastle University, and University Professor at Georgetown University in Washington, D.C.

IN THE LATENESS OF THE WORLD

BLOODAXE | £10.99 | PBS PRICE £8.25

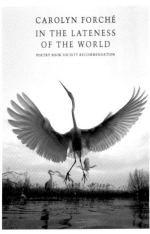

CAROLYN FORCHÉ
IN THE LATENESS
OF THE WORLD
POETRY BOOK SOCIETY RECOMMENDATION

In her memoir, *What You Have Heard is True*, Carolyn Forché recounts witnessing the start of El Salvador's civil war in the late 1970s as a poet and human rights worker. Her title refers to this act of witness, a shaping principle in Forché's poetic oeuvre, and to her most famous poem, 'The Colonel', which describes a tense and horrific scene at the home of an officer of the military junta. That poem, and others from her second collection, *The Country Between Us*, continue to stir readers today. Never perhaps since the mid-twentieth century has the abuse of power and the destruction of life, as well as hope, been more socially and politically relevant. These themes and the motifs of exile and justice have recurred throughout Forché's work since, often transmuted through the great witness of poets emerging from the turmoil of a previous century in Europe. *In the Lateness of the World*, her fifth book of poems after a hiatus of seventeen years, similarly meditates on questions of witness, displacement and war. Through poems touching on the refugee crisis, genocide, nationalist strongmen and climate emergency, Forché paints a bleak but accurate picture of the West's supposed postwar prosperity. Throughout this new collection, she turns her inimical, at times prophetic, eye onto a still new and unstable century. In 'The Last Puppet' we find the familiar (but always terrifying) subversions of free will. Taken politically in the tradition of dissent, the puppet offers a signal of hope.

> The puppet maker lifts it to the light and has it speak
>
> a language it will never speak again, its shadow finding the shadow
> on the wall of no one else. Then he puts a last song in its mouth.
>
> Souls have their own world. They are the descendants of clouds.
> Take this puppet to America. Hold it to the light.

Elsewhere there are intimate and timeless elegies, like the opening poem 'Museum of Stones', which is an avalanche of loss ending with "the stone that marked the path of the sun as it entered the human dawn." Other poems are for, or in memory of, figures as various as the poets Robert Creeley and Ilya Kaminsky and Leonel Gomez, who invited Forché to El Salvador so many decades ago, in conversation, as is the whole collection, with the past and an uncertain future.

18 SANDEEP PARMAR

CAROLYN FORCHÉ

In the Lateness of the World was written over a period of seventeen years, during the first two decades of the 21st century, poems arriving in clusters with silences between them as if no time had passed, language waking in a fitful state, as they are poems in a sense about the experience of time, written out of the temporal imagination, elegies in all senses and to everything, converging in an epoch of mourning and acknowledgement of irrevocable loss.

There is within them a litany of presences: friends and companions no longer alive, an archipelago of moments in a single human life, islands and cities, and also states of exilic being arising from a condition of global homelessness now and to come, a world of exiles and refugees within and without, poems having to do with bridges and ocean crossings, the debris fields of wars, survival in the aftermath and what it is like still to be alive to one's surprise. Other poets are mourned throughout but also honored for their gifts. It is the end, this book is whispering, but something else will come.

There are poems written in Indonesia and in Ireland, in Greece and Vietnam, India, childhood, an island in Puget Sound. There are lighthouses, seas, many species of birds, shadow puppets and water shortages, cemeteries, orchards, libraries, and the secrets of earlier life. So this is a deeply personal book, filled with disclosures. The dead and the living are together and everything happens at once. As the poet Melissanti wrote: "What has been and what is becoming are all of the same age."

CAROLYN RECOMMENDS

Philip Gross, *Between the Islands* (Bloodaxe Books); Alice Oswald, *Falling Awake* (Cape); Alice Oswald, *Nobody* (Cape); Anne Carson, *FLOAT* (Cape); *The Long Take*: a noir narrative by Robin Robertson (Cape); Sean O'Brien, *Europa* (Picador); Sinéad Morrissey, *On Balance* (Picador); Jennifer Militello, *A Camouflage of Specimens and Garments* (Tupelo); *Asymmetry: Poems by Adam Zagajewski* (Farrar, Straus and Giroux); Paula Meehan, *Geomantic* (Dedalus Press); Maram al-Masri, *Liberty Walks Naked*, translated by Theo Dorgan (Southword Editions); Ilya Kaminsky, *Deaf Republic* (Faber & Faber); Jericho Brown, *The Tradition* (Picador) and Patricia Smith, *Incendiary Art* (Bloodaxe).

RECOMMENDATION

to sleep like the flight of a crane through colorless dreams

Image: Zsolt Kudich

THE LIGHTKEEPER

A night without ships. Foghorns calling into walled cloud, and you
still alive, drawn to the light as if it were a fire kept by monks,
darkness once crusted with stars, but now death-dark as you sail inward.
Through wild gorse and sea wrack, through heather and torn wool
you ran, pulling me by the hand, so I might see this for once in my life:
the spin and spin of light, the whirring of it, light in search of the lost,
there since the era of fire, era of candles and hollow wick lamps,
whale oil and solid wick, colza and lard, kerosene and carbide,
the signal fires lighted on this perilous coast in the Tower of Hook.
You say to me, Stay awake, be like the lens maker who died with his
lungs full of glass, be the yew in blossom when bees swarm, be
their amber cathedral and even the ghosts of Cistercians will be kind to you.
In a certain light as after rain, in pearled clouds or the water beyond,
seen or sensed water, sea or lake, you would stop still and gaze out
for a long time. Also, when fireflies opened and closed in the pines,
and a star appeared, our only heaven. You taught me to live like this.
That after death it would be as it was before we were born. Nothing
to be afraid. Nothing but happiness as unbearable as the dread
from which it comes. Go toward the light always, be without ships.

DANEZ SMITH

Danez Smith is the author of *Don't Call Us Dead* (Chatto & Windus), winner of the Forward Prize for Best Collection, the Midwest Booksellers Choice Award, and a finalist for the National Book Award, and *[insert] boy* (YesYes Books, 2014), winner of the Kate Tufts Discovery Award and the Lambda Literary Award for Gay Poetry. They are the recipient of fellowships from the Poetry Foundation, the McKnight Foundation, the Montalvo Arts Center, Cave Canem, and the National Endowment for the Arts. Danez's work has been featured widely including on Buzzfeed, *The New York Times*, PBS NewsHour, Best American Poetry, *Poetry Magazine*, and on the Late Show with Stephen Colbert. Danez has been featured as part of Forbes' annual 30 Under 30 list and is the winner of a Pushcart Prize. They are a member of the Dark Noise Collective and co-host of VS with Franny Choi, a podcast sponsored by the Poetry Foundation and Postloudness.

HOMIE

CHATTO | £10.99 | PBS PRICE £8.25

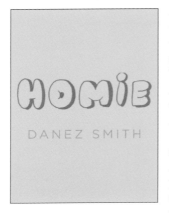

Danez Smith's *Homie* appears hot on the heels of their acclaimed *Don't Call Us Dead*. In some ways, this collection is reminiscent of the verbal energy and playfulness of their debut pamphlet *[insert boy]*. There is an attention to the politics and violence of America that will be familiar to readers on this side of the pond. A focus on spoken language, on speech itself, puts Smith in the realm of Amiri Baraka (whereas *Don't Call Us Dead* pointed to Ginsberg and Whitman). Less concerned with reaching out, *Homie* has the confidence of a poet whose work proceeds them, who is talking to an audience of admirers who get the references. Take the title, which isn't the book's actual title. "Homie", from "homeboy", is a way of indicating kinship, friendship between men, belonging (at least in my 1990s Californian register). It also, necessarily, suggests "home", those with whom you're at home and those who inevitably are not welcome. Broaden this to the US as a whole and you get an incisive discourse – a metaphor for Trump's nativist America where Immigration and Customs Enforcement (ICE, for those in the know) can un-home you and quite literally put you in a cage. There's genius here at work; language I struggle to relay here (because we aren't homies and words that recur throughout this collection rely on legitimately identifying with race and sexual identity and understanding) is precisely what this book means to explore for a particularly non-black or white readership.

> this ain't about language
> but who language holds
>
> those niggas who say my name
> like it's good news. i'm in love
>
> with purple gums, the yellow stain
> of front teeth, the bit of plaque
>
> unbrushed away revealed when
> my niggas laugh language...

What does it mean to unburden oneself from speaking to the majoritarian other? What possibilities might it provide for kinship – there are many family and love poems alongside the book's opening 'my president', where everyone from the speaker's mother to Rihanna is their president. And here we do actually encounter Whitman, Ginsberg and crucially Langston Hughes's singing: "i sing your names / sing your names / your names / my mighty anthem".

SANDEEP PARMAR

SELECTOR'S COMMENT

DANEZ SMITH

I didn't know I was writing *Homie / My Nig* until I went looking for it. I was trying to see if I had enough poems to gather up for a chapbook and realized I had been unknowingly drafting all these poems that moved through and around ideas of friendship, intimacy, and community. Part of this was due to mourning and missing a great friend of mine who had taken his own life and my reconciliation with his death and my own suicidal moods. The book fought me.

I had a difficult period of about a year of all these bad, corny poems that were trying to be about friendship instead of just allowing the power of that kind of love to enter, move, and transform the poems. I think I got close. The book is "about" more things than I intended, but I'm increasingly less interested in the "aboutness" of books. I want to know what a book "does" and if this book is doing it's little thing correctly it will inspire a few "I Love You" texts between friends and leave some thinking about how to love our communities, small and global, with greater intention.

The book pulls from my personal and collective memories, from canons of poets and rappers, trying to build something both highly personal to me, familiar or warm to my most beloved and urgent audiences, fun and deceptively dangerous. I think I could write this book three more times. There's another version that is more about portraiture, another that locates and images friendship's power through history, but here is my little diary of what I thought, what it felt like, and what love made it bearable as the living happened.

DANEZ RECOMMENDS

The wonderful Black poets who make up "The Detroit School" set a model for me as to what it looked like to be in loving community with other artists and how to be diverse kinds of excellent alongside peers. Three of those poets – Aricka Foreman, *Salt Body Shimmer*; Nandi Comer, *Tapping Out*; and Tommye Blount, *Fantasia for the Man in Blue* – all release debuts this year and the world could not be more blessed with the coming abundance.

RECOMMENDATION

25

HOMIE

DANEZ SMITH

I'M GOING BACK TO
MINNESOTA WHERE
SADNESS MAKES SENSE

o California, don't you know the sun is only a god
if you learn to starve for her? i'm over the ocean

i stood at its lip, dressed in down, praying for snow.
i know i'm strange, too much light makes me nervous

at least in this land where the trees always bear green.
i know something that doesn't die can't be beautiful.

have you ever stood on a frozen lake, California?
the sun above you, the snow & stalled sea—a field of mirror

all demanding to be the sun, everything around you
is light & it's gorgeous & if you stay too long it will kill you.

it's so sad, you know? you're the only warm thing for miles
the only thing that can't shine.

DANEZ SMITH

MARVIN THOMPSON

Marvin Thompson was born in London to Jamaican parents and now teaches English to secondary school children in mountainous south Wales. He has an MA in Creative Writing and was one of three poets selected by The Poetry School and Nine Arches Press for the Primers 2 mentoring scheme. His work has appeared in *The Poetry Review, Poetry Wales* and *Red*, and in 2019, his magical-realist war poem, 'The Many Reincarnations of Gerald, Oswald Archibald Thompson' was submitted by *Long Poem Magazine* for the Forward Prize for Best Poem. *Road Trip* is his first full length collection.

ROAD TRIP

PEEPAL TREE | £9.99 | PBS PRICE £7.50

Marvin Thompson is plucky in writing long poems, or sequences of poems when they're tough to publish. Every detail earns its place; short lines, matching their sense-units, provide a way of writing and remembering carefully – especially when it comes to the poet's father, who served in the army:

> It took me two years
>
> to free myself
> from uncertainty
>
> and believe
> my memories;

Gradually the reader is convinced that such precision, and timing, is absolutely necessary – there are so many micro-achievements to savour, such as the deconstruction, for instance, of the idiom "I'm cool with it". Details preserved in verse, as in amber, paradoxically gesture toward the transience of our lives, and the dominant mode is that of mental drift, where painful memories resurface beyond the speaker's control. If there are moments when "thoughts flow", from one thing to another, this may be a creative opportunity but also a traumatic associativeness difficult to weather.

This virtuosic book also reveals the poet's skill with a longer, democratic-feeling, grittily capacious line – "Rain falls knuckle-hard on the giant arms of a brass Chartist"– and contains sonnets as well as ambitious poems in personae. Born in London to Jamaicans, Campbell now lives in Wales, and through poetic form he discovers entry-points into multiple histories:

> There's a documentary with only nine views
> that explains how the N-word spawned from a need
> to dehumanise people of a dark hue
> so cotton profits would feel less like greed
> or sin. The word's history is not well-known.

This is a poet who writes about complex things clearly – in heartfelt, often personal, but also investigative, and ever-dexterous, structures. The poems are clever, cutting and empathetic, and I wish there were space to quote more.

SELECTOR'S COMMENT

VIDYAN RAVINTHIRAN

MARVIN THOMPSON

I feel oddly compelled to explain why I choose *Road Trip* as the title for my debut poetry collection. The fact is, I am incapable of writing a sequence of poems without a car journey being involved in the narrative. Yes, I've turned a strange inadequacy into a structural conceit! Outings to Southend on Sea or south London to see cousins and aunties were the source of much childhood joy. My fictional journeys tap into these boyhood pleasures.

As much as I am an advocate for form and narrative, both these elements hampered the first phase of my writing career. Hooked on sonnets, I regularly tried to corset complex stories into fourteen lines. The resulting poems were left unpublished.

The daredevil in me has always tried to push traditional literary boundaries. This desire manifested itself in years of soggy writing in which I avoided the themes of identity and race – as a Black poet, I thought not writing about these topics was subversive. Then I moved to Wales. With my life in London gone, there was no one on hand to discuss issues pertaining to my Blackness. Loneliness ensued.

Les Twins (French brothers who fuse hip-hop and contemporary dance styles) are currently one of the biggest influences on my writing; they embody my love of music and narrative. Their dreadlocks and afros remind me how I got through my cultural isolation in south Wales: I wrote poems about being Black.

Before leaving for night shifts on a psychiatric ward in north London, my mum would read to my brothers and I. Her renditions of Anansi stories in Jamaican patois were wondrous. Now, for my children, Anansi is Santa's chief helper and the guy who gives them 50p when their teeth fall out. Just like with my use of sonnets, sestinas and villanelles, I have given British traditions a remix.

Each time I've tried to write a lyric poem, I've failed. In prayer, I thank God for these failures. Writing narrative poems has allowed me to reminisce over once forgotten road trips. Lush!

MARVIN RECOMMENDS

Les Twins; Octavia Butler, *The Parable of the Sower and The Parable of the Talents* (Headline); Patience Agbabi, *Bloodshot Monochrome* (Cannongate); Bernardine Evaristo, *Lara* (Bloodaxe); Anthony Anaxagorou, *After the Formalities* (Penned in the Margins); Raymond Antrobus, *The Perseverance* (Penned in the Margins); Jane Commane, *Assembly Lines* (Bloodaxe); Mary Jean Chan, *Flèche* (Faber); Roger Robinson, *A Portable Paradise* (Peepal Tree); *H.D. Selected Poems* (New Directions); Mario Petrucci, *Heavy Water* (Enitharmon) and *The New Yorker* Fiction Podcast.

Road Trip
Marvin Thompson

AN INTERVIEW WITH COMEDY GENIUS OLIVIER WELSH

3. What's the truth about how Tommy Mann was born?

2016 was a year of pain,
'Muslims go home!' spat from once-shy mouths.
Like Enoch Powell, Brexit turned tongues profane.
We were not so much divided by north and south
but by politicians' poisonous, post-truth views.
Have I Got News For You hosted my protest
of ironic racist quips in Gramps' royal blue,
a jacket Tommy wore with a puffed chest.

Tommy's first pub gig? I choked with fright.
His smoking jacket dripped with punters' spit
and his barbs about refugees' bums were booed.
So I studied, gave his voice more plum, more bite
and learnt his swagger: Tommy's path was lit.
To date on YouTube? Nine billion views.

SRINIVAS RAYAPROL

Srinivas Rayaprol was born in 1925 in Secunderabad. He studied in Nizam College, Hyderabad, and at the Banaras Hindu University before going to Stanford University, where he obtained an M.S. in Civil Engineering. While in the US he started writing poetry in English and interacted closely with writers like William Carlos Williams, Yvor Winters, and James Laughlin. His correspondence with Williams has been published as *Why Should I Write a Poem Now: The Letters of Srinivas Rayaprol and William Carlos Williams, 1949-1958* (2018), edited by Graziano Krätli. His books of poetry include *Bones and Distances* (1968), *Married Love and Other Poems* (1972) and *Selected Poems* (1995). He died in 1998.

ANGULAR DESIRE: SELECTED POEMS

CARCANET | £16.99 | PBS PRICE £12.75

For decades, modernist revision has made much of reclaiming authors from the margins of the twentieth-century canon. This has more often been the work of feminist scholars looking for forgotten literary mothers in the print rooms, magazines and café terraces in the shadows of the Pound-Eliot-Joyce nexus. Race and colonial diaspora Anglophone writers in the mid century are slowly being added to the redrawing of modernism – an umbrella term for aesthetic experiments roughly falling between 1890 and 1940. Srinivas Rayaprol is one of these figures, though his poetic output is somewhat later and his writing has largely appeared in editions published in India. This critical edition, compiled and introduced by Graziano Krätli and Vidyan Ravinthiran, has much to tell us about an expanded view of modernist poetry globally and temporally into the 1960s and 70s. Take, for instance, Rayaprol's engagement with American poets during his time living and writing in the US, whose names are the dedicatees and influences for many of these poems: William Carlos Williams, Ezra Pound, the sculptor Constantin Brâncuși, Picasso, etc. Rayaprol corresponded with Williams who encouraged him to write – and evidence of this is found here with one of William's most famous poems being invoked ('This is Just to Say', the poem confessing eating plums that has launched a thousand internet memes).

> I do not grieve every time
> There is a death in the street
> But a man died today
> Whom I last saw placing a rose
> In his button-hole.

Instead of plums we get roses, invoking another modernist poet Gertrude Stein ("a rose is a rose is a rose"). The imagistic lightness and sparseness of Rayaprol's writing is present throughout the book. Elsewhere there's a neo-Victorian sentimentality that, as Ravinthiran's excellent introduction points out, is a function of a colonial discourse and the inescapability of the English poet for Indian writers. Reflections on India, to which he would return later in life, as well as family and his own sexuality make for a broad and thoughtful volume – and one that is necessary to the readjustments of canon formation and assumptions about writers from the former colonies.

SANDEEP PARMAR

SELECTOR'S COMMENT

10 DOWNING STREET

I saw a few books in a pub
the other day
calico-bound volumes on a mahogany shelf
over a marble mantelpiece

10 Downing Street it's called
with a picture of Churchill
proudly displayed
over the bound books

A pitcher of beer and some crisps later
I walk over to see the titles
of the attractive books
Unimaginative titles by
nondescript authors
that you'd find in British clubs
of the old Cantonment days
or in P & O liners on the high seas

but there's a volume of Cyril Connolly
to surprise me, and a few poems by
second rate poets, for a change
2000 watts of power beats the music
of today flickering between the lights
to drown out the frail voice
of a Swedish singer

which surfaces now and then by intent

Is this the India that I have come back to?
—tempted by Gandhi's gospel and Nehru's call
after centuries of slavery. Have we come to this?
Bound by the shackles that we overthrew not so long ago.

CHRISTEL WIINBLAD

Christel Wiinblad was born in 1980 in Svendborg, Denmark. She has published four collections of poetry; 49 *Forelskelser* (2008), *Min lillebror – en morgen i himlen, ihvertfald i det grønne* (2008), *Det ligner en sorg* (2011) and *Sommerlys* (2013), and three novels; *Prolog* (2011), *Ingen åbner* (2012) and *De elskende* (2014).

Malene Engelund was born in 1980 in Aalborg, Denmark. She moved to England in 2002 and holds an MA in Creative Writing from Royal Holloway University of London. She is co-editor of the Days of Roses poetry anthologies and was highly commended in the Faber New Poets 2013/14 competition. Her debut pamphlet *The Wild Gods* was published by Valley Press in 2016.

MY LITTLE BROTHER

TRANSLATED BY MALENE ENGELUND

VALLEY PRESS | £7.99 | PBS PRICE £6.00

As always it has been a very difficult choice but I have gone for the Danish poet, Christel Wiinblad's *My Little Brother*, translated by Marlene Engelund. The book is something of a miracle in that it consists entirely of a series of precisely dated poems about the life and death of Wiinblad's troubled younger brother at the age of twenty-two in 2006. The poems are quite long, simple in language, essentially narrative, without simile or metaphor, the whole loving, but entirely without sentimentality, bearing the weight of loss with grace and apparent ease as through a clear glass, yet piercingly moving. Sometimes it seemed as much account as verse but the rhythm and phrasing of Engelund's excellent translation is entirely persuasive. For all those reasons it is difficult to quote tellingly but here she finds her brother in a wood:

> that the dog lifted its heavy ears
> because it could hear
> the faint ringing
> from the spot inside the woods
>
> and it lifted its nose
> to the air as if to the stumbling lonely figure,
> there a bit further ahead so pale and grey
> that it was almost blue

Where does life end and poetry begin? How does one ghost the other? There were many fine books available this quarter but not one like this. There are the selected poems of Mila Haugová, translated by James Sutherland-Smith, compact, precise and beautiful; the marvellous dark narrative quatrains of the Albanian Gëzim Hajdari, set in the period of dictatorship, translated by Ian Seed; there is the great Alejandra Pizarnik; Manuel Vilas with excellent translations by James Womack; and Charlotte Van Den Broeck's sparkling *Chameleon | Nachtroer*, translated by David Colmer. And more. I heartily recommend all these since they all enrich our sense of the world and expand the possibilities of poetry and of translation. All good poetry translation does that. The best translation is poetry itself, a poetry that strikes us as new, born out of the language of elsewhere that is also the world in which we live.

GEORGE SZIRTES

1: MY LITTLE BROTHER

He's wearing his light blue overalls and the t-shirt with navy-blue and bottle-green stripes. He's all light and looks like a small warm flame or a paper angel that smells of child and only faintly of piss. You can't tell that he's thinking of all the things the bushes whispered to him that morning while I could only hear their soft movements in the wind.

He's on my lap pulling his face into the most manic expressions he knows. Outside the camera's reach, most of his Playmobil Eskimos are spread across the floor, the majority of them decapitated, and one of the igloos has broken into five pieces because he dropped it when, eagerly looking for someone to show the new village, he fell over the door frame and landed in the middle of the settlement like an improbable catastrophe, scraping his palms and his knees.

I can tell by my face above his, and by my arms holding him in that tight big-sisterly grip, that just before my mum pressed the release and the flash went off, I could feel the small fingers on his left hand press into my thigh and I can tell that I'm struggling to hold back the laughter, consumed with pride and a feral joy.

Only now do I notice that you can already see it, how in this photo too he frowns and tightens his lips in that unusual pose that I now know means he's disturbed by something that'll never be spoken because he's entirely alone with something that can't be spoken. Only in twenty and a half years (now yesterday) will he get close to vocalising it, and at that time when it's finally revealed, this is the expression he'll carry, because again he'll try his best to keep the terror of what's just happened at bay, because desperate and lost to himself, he's finally gathered enough courage to try to make it stop.

Image: Koen Potgieter

SÍOFRA McSHERRY

Based in Berlin, Síofra McSherry was born in Newry, Northern Ireland. She earned her PhD in American Literature from the Freie Universität Berlin in 2017. Síofra completed a BA in English at the University of Oxford and received her MA from University College London. She has published her poems in anthologies including *The Salt Book of Younger Poets* (Salt, 2011), *Bird Book* (Sidekick Books, 2011), *Sylvia is Missing* (Flarestack, 2012) and journals including *Poetry Wales, Poems in Which, Foam:e, Abraxas* and *Hysteria*. *Requiem* is her debut pamphlet.

REQUIEM

THE EMMA PRESS | £5.00

In *Requiem*, Síofra McSherry presents twelve poems in memory of her mother. As she notes at the beginning of the work, the sequence roughly follows the structure of the Requiem Mass (to which she helpfully provides a key, and which in itself works as a type of found poem). To this she adds elements of classical myth and Irish folk song, and the whole makes for an unforgettable mix of unsentimental reportage, gothic wit, and exuberant fortitude.

The figure of Death is personified throughout the sequence, a fedora-wearing intruder, "all clatter / and tooth, as generous with his grins / as with all else." McSherry enjoys the possibilities of this so much that Death appears as though he's just walked out of a Tim Burton film: "His legs were thin / as candy canes and his jaw was startlingly defined." In the same poem, the wider family suffer his unnerving presence:

> To make things worse we kept finding things he'd left
> in every room, empty bottles of cheap imported
> beer, a pack of playing cards with all the queens
> missing, an annotated copy of Pope's *Essay on Man*,
> papier-mâché Día de los Muertos figurines that clashed
> with the décor, which was mostly magnolia
> and terracotta, a country farmhouse theme, with oak.

Elsewhere, the ritual of repetitions allows McSherry to construct contemporary prayers:

> Gastrostomy have mercy upon her
> Citalopram have mercy upon her
> Riluzole have mercy upon her
> Morphine have mercy upon her

Throughout, McSherry walks the line between the living and the dead; honouring the imperfections and foibles of the former, acknowledging the enduring complexities of the latter. She manages to accommodate the wide-scale import of the Requiem Mass and its associated religious world-view (often the focus of her iconoclastic and satiric impulses) while never losing sight of the human subject at its centre.

SELECTOR'S COMMENT

A.B. JACKSON & DEGNA STONE

1. INTROITUS

AD TE OMNIS CARO VENIET

To you all flesh shall come
and before you all flesh shall cave.
Witness the bleed-out
of desire, the avalanche of synapses,
the extinction of the will. Unprepared
we shall wake to your all-blinding light,

we who carried flashlights and thought
we knew the sun. Your veils
shall set fast our limbs,
swaddle our mouths and noses, our eyes
and ears and skin. We shall speak nothing,
hear nothing, see nothing. Nothing shall be known.

Before you sense is scattered and meaning lies in ruin.
Before you come none willingly
and from you shall go none.
Hear our prayer.

JENNIFER WONG

Jennifer Wong was born and grew up in Hong Kong, and is the author of two poetry collections including *Goldfish* (Chameleon Press, 2013). She studied English at Oxford and received an MA in Creative Writing at the University of East Anglia. She is the recipient of the Hong Kong Young Artist Award (Literary Arts) and earned a PhD on the idea of place and identity in Asian diaspora poetry from Oxford Brookes University. Her work has appeared in various journals including *The Rialto, Poetry London, Poetry Review, And Other Poems, Oxford Poetry, Stand, North, Wildness, Cha, Wasafiri, Voice & Verse, Warwick Review* and others. She won the runner-up prize at the Bi'an Writers Awards and was long-listed in the National Poetry Competition.

LETTERS HOME

NINE ARCHES PRESS | £9.99 | PBS PRICE £7.50

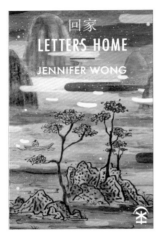

James Baldwin prophetically observed in his 1956 novel *Giovanni's Room* that "perhaps home is not a place but simply an irrevocable condition." Jennifer Wong's *Letters Home* explores similar sentiments, a state of being which unpacks an array of intertwined worlds through carefully positioned language, family and a series of cultural relationships. The poems contain an unwavering sense of wanting to feel affiliated with a perceived homeland, yet one understood as being distant and unavailable – the often-compromised identities which result after a history of colonialism and forced migration have been experienced. In 'Monarch Butterfly' the speaker tells us "Neither do I / know after all these years / if I am a Chinese girl / who hasn't returned home // or a girl from Hong Kong / who has stayed in England." The poem's speakers often appear conflicted while wanting to preserve various cultural practices in hostile or indifferent spaces. At odds with notions of home and belonging the collection also alludes to the British occupation of Hong Kong and the treatment of its citizens.

> A self-declared king for fifty years, painting
> all over the colony—a city where the British
> lived like paradise birds on mid-levels
> and the Chinese sweated, selling meats
> in wet markets but Oh! the freedom to
> march and shout to do what you did!

A constant desire to pin the idea of "home" to one place seems impossible, which in the mind of the speakers appears to diminish, as in the poem 'To Su Li Zhen' where we're told:

> The cure for homesickness
> is to resist falling in love
> with the city...

The desire to resist becoming attached to a foreign place through the possible fear of losing or having one's identity erased, is a strong and central theme throughout this important work.

ANTHONY ANAXAGOROU

SELECTOR'S COMMENT

JENNIFER WONG

回家 is not a literal translation of the English title. Rather, it suggests "returning home". For someone who inhabits multiple languages, there is constantly an uneasy gap, a sense of instability, of guesswork, or a leap of faith. Ágnes Heller, a Hungarian philosopher, describes home as a place where "no footnotes are needed". What can be understood and what remains untranslated? Sometimes, one doesn't know which way is home. What's home: a location? A country? A shared dream or language?

I am intrigued by the idea of time-travel and space-travel, the impossibility to map the "origin" of an individual. From the story of an ice-lantern, a derelict village school in Guizhou to the graffiti and tear gas in Hong Kong's streets, these poems reveal glimpses into memories etched into skin, the fragments of different cultural, historical and linguistic worlds; the power hierarchies and matrix of expectations and beliefs which shape, confine, trouble, liberate me.

I want to explore and embed what history means, the sheer weight of lack and longing for those who try to unravel the complexities of who they are and where or what they come from. These complexities speak not just to migrants, sojourners and refugees, but all of us. For history lies in our core being, and embodies an unending voyage of border-crossing. It begins in the past but overlaps with the present and the future. I long for a poetic language that transcends borders and censorship, one that embraces dialects and cultures, speaks with sympathy and sincerity.

JENNIFER RECOMMENDS

Zeina Hashem Beck, *Louder Than Hearts* (Bauhan); Hannah Lowe, *The Neighbourhood* (Outspoken Press); John McCullough, *Reckless Paper Birds* (Penned in the Margins); Anne Carson, *FLOAT* (Cape); Rebecca Goss, *Girl* (Carcanet); Hannah Sullivan, *Three Poems* (Faber); Anne Marie Fyfe, *No Far Shore, Charting Unknown Waters* (Seren); Mary Jean Chan, *Flèche* (Faber); João Luís Barreto de Guimarães, *NOMAD*; Kevin Maynard (trans.), *The Iron Flute: War Poetry from Ancient and Medieval China* (Arc); Jacqueline Saphra, *Dad, Remember You Are Dead* (Nine Arches Press); Sarah Westcott, *Slant Light* (Pavilion Poetry); Ilya Kaminsky, *Deaf Republic* (Faber); David Clarke, *The Europeans* (Nine Arches Press); Kathryn Maris, *The House with Only an Attic and a Basement* (Penguin); Tracy K. Smith, *Wade in the Water* (Penguin); Denise Riley, *Say Something Back* (Picador); Marilyn Chin, *A Portrait of the Self as Nation* (W.W. Norton); Sally Wen Mao, *Oculus* (Graywolf Press); Morgan Parker, *Magical Negro* (Tin House); Mona Arshi, *Dear Big Gods* (Pavilion Poetry); Jeremy Noel Todd, (ed.) *The Penguin Book of the Prose Poem*; Laura Scott, *So Many Rooms* (Carcanet) and Anthony Anaxagorou, *After the Formalities* (Penned in the Margins).

MSLEXIA & PBS
WOMEN'S POETRY COMPETITION
WINNERS

1ST PRIZE	REGI CLAIRE
2ND PRIZE	JACQUELINE SAPHRA
3RD PRIZE	ALEX TOMS
UNPUBLISHED POET PRIZE	ERIN COPPIN
FINALISTS	ELOISE BIRTWHISTLE
	MARLO BESTER-SPROUL
	PENNY BOXALL
	CHARLOTTE BUCKLEY
	BECKY CHERRIMAN
	MICHAELA COPLEN
	NICOLA DALY
	CLAIRE DYER
	KATIE HALE
	LEAH LARWOOD
	WENDY ORR
	ILSE PEDLER
	KATE POTTS
	SUSAN UTTING
	J.S. WATTS
	SARAH WIMBUSH

ABOUT THE JUDGE

MALIKA BOOKER is a British poet of Guyanese and Grenadian parentage and the founder of Malika's Poetry Kitchen. Her collection *Pepper Seed* (Peepal Tree Press) was shortlisted for the OCM Bocas Prize and the Seamus Heaney Centre prize. Malika was the first British poet to be a fellow at Cave Canem and the inaugural Poet in Residence at the Royal Shakespeare Company. She has written for the stage and radio, and her poems were published in *Out of Bounds: Black & Asian Poets* (Bloodaxe, 2012) and *Ten: Poets of the New Generation* (Bloodaxe, 2010). In 2017 she was shortlisted for the Forward Prize for Best Single Poem.

THE JUDGE'S REPORT

The winning poem '(Un)certainties' by Regi Claire is a harrowing interrogation of a grievous tragedy using the structure of a multiple-choice form. The formal constraints provide a never-ending relentless repetition and rendition that traps the reader in the unfolding narrative. This obsessive, risky long poem dares the reader to leave the poem unaffected and unscarred. It is not your usual competition poem yet I could not help but marvel at the poem's tenaciousness. Its plain factual language a natural counterpoint to the haziness of the actual recount of the sister's drowning. The poem became the yardstick against which the other poems paled. There is something so forceful about the way the narrative and formal structure fit, about the bravery of the entry into a competition that can only invite this type of award, even considering the flaws of the narrative breaks where I feel the dramatic asides could have been edited so that the reader remains trapped in the multiple choice hell, yet there is something utterly stunning about the tight constraint contrasted against the sprawling prose.

Jacqueline Saphra's 'Fishwife', the second place poem, is structurally composed around such visceral and guttural sonic quality, that I found myself uttering lines from the poem over and over, delighting in the rhythmic sharpness of the words, yet haunted by the lyric's narrative drive. This seemingly literal tale is as layered and brutal as any Grimm's brothers, as alluded to in the epigram. The poem responds to the fishwife's anger (epigram), by illuminating the premeditated action this anger initiates. The couplets demonstrate that this is a poet who clearly understands how to manipulate language as illustrated by the way the alliterative rhythm pushes against the taut syntax, and is reined in by rigid couplets and line breaks.

'Daedalus in Therapy' by Alex Toms, is the beautifully written third placed poem. The lyric's power lies in the contrast between two voices, the mythical character Daedalus and his therapist, whose italicised voice prompts the narrative forward. The poet humanizes Daedalus's troubled figure, by situating him in a therapy session. There is a realism here that is both vulnerable and revealing. The alluring language, and metaphorical attention to detail gives this poem its power and made me engage with it again and again, luxuriating in lines like: "A blur of white… beating like a moth or a belly… radiant like the harvest moon."

'Kindling' by Erin Coppin wins the prize for the best poem by an unpublished poet with this sparse powerful poem that hinges on a shocking volta-like turn in the thirteenth line. Coppin uses alliteration throughout the poem to illuminate the ordinary scene of a woman lighting a fire. Yet rightly abandons all poetic lyricism for the stark admission in line fourteen: "I have not felt the baby move in days," providing a shocking pathos, that blindsides, shifting the obsessive description of the fire into an extended metaphor for worrying or loss.

Read the rest of Malika Booker's Judge's Report at www.poetrybooks.co.uk

| MALIKA BOOKER

(UN)CERTAINTIES
AN EXTRACT

My sister once gave me
A. an ultramarine silk scarf
B. a star-shaped candlestick of clear glass
C. a guardian angel made from clay and driftwood

My sister loved
A. her family
B. her partner
C. kayaks

My sister's partner loved
A. her
B. his family
C. kayaks

My sister and her partner loved
A. adventure
B. sports
C. water
D. the sea

My sister and her partner
A. had been on sea kayaking trips before
B. were familiar with that coastline
C. were offered a guided tour
D. trusted their abilities and experience

My sister sent her children
A. a WhatsApp message saying how excited she was about
                                 that day's 10 km kayaking trip
B. a picture of the mirror-smooth sea
C. a selfie in a swim vest
D. emojis of dolphins

My sister's postcard to our parents
A. was sent before the kayaking trip
B. was sent by hotel staff after the kayaking trip
C. arrived ten days after the kayaking trip, before her funeral

My sister died
A. on Friday 13th
B. on Saturday 14th

My sister's partner did not die
A. on Friday 13th
B. on Saturday 14th

My sister died at sea, alone
A. soon after sunset in a storm
B. in the dark in a storm
C. at dawn, after a storm
D. in sunlight, on the morning after a storm

My sister's partner clung to his kayak at sea, alone
A. from sunset to false dawn throughout a storm
B. from sunset to sunrise throughout a storm and the calm hours beyond
C. from sunset to sunlit morning throughout a storm and the calm hours beyond

Read the full poem and all the winners at www.poetrybooks.co.uk

REGI CLAIRE is a Swiss-born novelist and short fiction writer based in Edinburgh, Scotland. She writes in English, although her mother tongue is Swiss German. Her publications include two novels (*The Waiting* and *The Beauty Room*) and two story collections (*Fighting It* and *Inside-Outside*). She has twice been shortlisted for Saltire Scottish Book of the Year awards, longlisted for the Edge Hill Prize and MIND Book of the Year. She won 1st prize in the Edinburgh Review 10th Anniversary Short Story Competition. She teaches at Edinburgh City Art Centre and Edinburgh University.

1ST PRIZE WINNER

SPRING BOOK REVIEWS

This sixth collection by an outstanding poet and playwright, who was recently shortlisted for the Ted Hughes and T.S. Eliot awards, takes its title from the poet's own invention of "The Air Year: the anniversary prior to paper". Bird surveys love and life with compelling wit and "a feedback form asking how I'd rate my life (very good, good, average, bad, very bad)". *The Air Year* is surreal and satirical but beneath all this levity, lies a candid vulnerability.

CARCANET | £9.99 | PBS PRICE £7.50

CHARLOTTE VAN DEN BROECK: CHAMELEON | NACHTROER
TRANSLATED BY DAVID COLMER

The first ever English translation of this innovative Belgian performance poet combines two collections into one volume. These subversive and shape-shifting poems journey through coming-of-age to heartbreak, dissolution and displacement. Sequences of Lethe-like waters flow throughout this luminous and questioning collection: "I am a place that doesn't exist / a place light pushes through".

BLOODAXE | £12.00 | PBS PRICE £9.00

COLETTE BRYCE: THE M PAGES

At the heart of this new collection by the award-winning poet Colette Bryce is a moving memorial, addressed to "M", a sibling who has suddenly died. Bryce poignantly explores the experience of unexpected bereavement and the difficulty of trying "to cast in words the unbelievable fact". This unflinching sequence moves through the sudden surrealness of loss and the corporeal horror of death ("one / cannot bear so much reality") to come to terms with our own mortality.

PICADOR | £10.99 | PBS PRICE   £8.25

RISHI DASTIDAR: SAFFRON JACK

A bold, formally challenging narrative poem, *Saffron Jack* alludes to a flag of the narrator's making: "a giant Union Jack. Except that it is saffron and gold and red and brown and green". This is the flag of a micro-nation which the poet forges from a warzone, carving a space in which the dispossessed and the disillusioned might achieve self-determination. What begins as a flight of ironic fantasy, hued by war and racism, becomes a rollicking damnation of hypocrisy, exclusion, racial violence and othering in the UK.

NINE ARCHES PRESS | £9.99 | PBS PRICE £7.50

MINA GORJI: ART OF ESCAPE

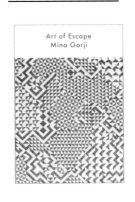

Gorji begins this fine collection in the manner of ecological samples – wasps and oak-apples, armadillos and dandelions – before a deft side-step to migrant experiences, abandoned homes, broken lives. This allusion places both within a sort of clinical scrutiny, in which human life is situated within an overwhelming bio-historical system. This is not to say *Art of Escape* is impersonal; Gorji's poems are concise but evocative, holding within them a painful beauty, a love of that which is uprooted, ignored and unappreciated.

CARCANET | £9.99 | PBS PRICE £7.50

PHILIP GROSS: BETWEEN THE ISLANDS

Sea and ocean, the liminality of shorelines, the psycho-geography of the coast (and all that it signifies) feature prominently in this contemplative new offering from the celebrated and prolific poet Philip Gross. Moving from island to island, continent to continent, *Between the Islands* is concerned with memories, with resonances throughout time, but also with emergent dangers; ecological fears and the rising islands of refuse accumulating in our oceans.

BLOODAXE | £10.99 | PBS PRICE £8.25

BOOK REVIEWS

SPRING BOOK REVIEWS

DAVID HARSENT: LOSS

Recent T.S. Eliot Prize winner David Harsent presents his thirteenth volume of poems with characterstic eloquence and formal mastery. Documenting the dead hours of the night with an insomniac's prophetic clarity, this is a sonorous sequence of sleeplessness and dream fragments which start and end at midnight: "It is 00:00 and the full of the night yet to come". Memories, recurring visions and "reckonings of loss" surface throughout this significant addition to Harsent's distinguished oeuvre.

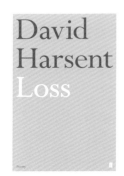

FABER | £14.99 (HB) | PBS PRICE £11.25

EVAN JONES: LATER EMPERORS

Canadian poet Evan Jones brings to life the human drama of history, lending a fragile humanity to great (and not so great) historic figures, "the Empire is not the emperor". From Roman Emperors Maximin and Gordian to the Byzantine chronicler Anna Komnene, each sequence voices vast swathes of ancient history. Beneath these vivid retellings Jones examines the dubious art of writing history itself, "don't unwrite what I've written", and the lessons we, and our own modern day emperors, can learn from the past.

CARCANET | £9.99 | PBS PRICE £7.50

RUTH PADEL: BEETHOVEN VARIATIONS

Beethoven Variations is a biography in verse – not only of Beethoven himself, but of Padel and her life-long connection to his music. Adroitly composed, this collection reflects upon the way music (and art in general) shapes both the creator and their audience, reverberating in ways neither could predict. Beautifully written and deeply engaging, *Beethoven Variations* is a wonderful read for enthusiasts of both Padel and Beethoven, or for those new to both artists.

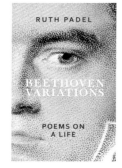

CHATTO & WINDUS | £12.00 | PBS PRICE £9.00

DON PATERSON: ZONAL

Paterson claims "All the poems in this collection take their imaginative cue from the first season of *The Twilight Zone*". This sets the tone for a collection which is part high-concept science-fictional experiment, part tongue-in-cheek unreliable autobiography, with Paterson at his playful best. *Zonal* avoids sliding into pretensions with an acute self-deprecatory humour. The overall effect is surprisingly candid; a sharp portrayal of what it is to live in a world saturated with information and popular culture, with competing zones of reality and unreality.

FABER | £14.99 (HB) | PBS PRICE £11.25

ANNE STEVENSON: COMPLETING THE CIRCLE

Originally named *Elegies and Celebrations, Completing the Circle* is a perfectly-composed journey through life and death. Astute and witty, Stevenson delivers memorable verse to live by: "without a wine of the mind, most poems are plonk, // without poetry, wine just makes you drunk." Just the right amount of humour offsets what would otherwise be profoundly sad – many of the poems are dedicated to lost peers – and so *Completing the Circle* provides a perfect philosophical companion for the trials of ageing.

BLOODAXE | £10.99 | PBS PRICE £8.25

ALEJANDRA PIZARNIK: DIANA'S TREE
TRANSLATED BY ANNA DEENY MORALES

This dual language Spanish translation sheds new light on a groundbreaking 1962 collection by the Argentinian poet Alejandra Pizarnik. Described by Octavio Paz as "a verbal crystallization formed by... ardent insomnia and dazzling clarity", *Diana's Tree* is haunted by death and "immersed / in the silence of things". Always circling emptiness and grief, Pizarnik's pared-down poems are perfectly poised in their search for light: "I have placed my body alongside the light / and sung of the sadness of the born."

SHEARSMAN | £9.95 | PBS PRICE £7.47

SPRING PAMPHLETS

IAN GLASS: ABOUT LEAVING

This deceptively simple pamphlet poignantly explores the process of coming to terms with the departure and, later, death of a loved one. Glass's poems move through sparse spaces of domestic absence, "Walking from one empty room to another, / filled with silence", towards acceptance, "it's time to walk away: close the door on the quiet room". Carrying the weight of love and loss, these poems offer hope of a new found strength, "You don't worry about tomorrow / you don't feel alone".

V.   PRESS | £6.50 |

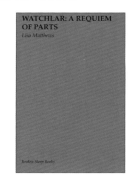

GAIL McCONNELL: FOTHERMATHER

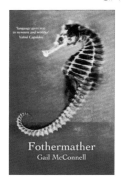

A sequence of experimental verse forms engaging with the matter of queer parentage in Northern Ireland, *Fothermather* is a playful and intriguing venture into understanding identity when one parent is separated from traditional biological parenthood. Enter the role of "fothermather" – that which is not entirely father or mother, but something of both, something different. With this neologism McConnell literally scores out tired Freudian assertions: "~~I cannot think of any need in childhood as strong as the need for a father's protection.~~"

INK   SWEAT   &   TEARS | £7.50 |

LISA MATTHEWS: WATCHLAR: A REQUIEM OF PARTS

Broken Sleep Books brings Lisa Matthews's masterful innovations to life in this micro pamphlet of photo-art and words. Described as "Phoetry" these photo poems, "mirror fold diptychs" and collaged "maquettes", are full of eeire displacements and doublings. Art and words merge and splinter in a sequence of "stones that float" and deepening forests. At times geometric, at others playful, *Watchlar* observes and disrupts the world around us.

BROKEN   SLEEP   BOOKS | £6.00

JASMINE SIMMS: LIKE HORSES

This confident and compelling debut charts the process of growing up, of a rural childhood and teenage years, gaining an education and finding one's place in the world. Simms's verse is compact but eloquent, demonstrating a keen eye which cuts through the everyday, weighing and measuring daily experience and casting it in new and revealing light. Simms's future work will be keenly anticipated.

SMITH | DOORSTOP | £5.00 |

KATHARINE TOWERS: THE VIOLIN FOREST

The award-winning poet Katharine Towers's latest pamphlet composes "a green thought", finely attuned to nature. Drawing inspiration from Boethius to Sibelius, Towers explores the forests which provide the "heartwood of violins". Her poems sing with mythic resonance but also seek the "soily heart of it all". From a "blackbird's fado" to a dead fox "stopped mid-pirouette" she captures the music of nature itself.

The Violin Forest

Katharine Towers

HAPPENSTANCE | £5.00 |

AMINA JAMA: A WARNING TO THE HOUSE THAT HOLDS ME

A Warning to the House that Holds Me is an exercise in breaking down boundaries; inter-personal, inter-continental, intersectional. Jama situates this sequence within the life of Frida Kahlo, plays this life in reverse, and then contrasts with her own experiences. This invites a rich concoction of influences: cultural touchstones from Somalia and Muslim faith; poetic responses to the works of Safia Ehillo, Ocean Vuong, Hera Lindsay Bird and two Netflix interludes. Altogether this makes for an electrifying mix, barely contained within these pages.

FLIPPED   EYE | £4.00 |

PAMPHLET REVIEWS

SPRING LISTINGS

NEW BOOKS

AUTHOR	TITLE	PUBLISHER	RRP
William Bedford	The Dancers of Colbek	Two Rivers Press	£9.99
Caroline Bird	The Air Year	Carcanet	£9.99
Daragh Breen	Nostoc	Shearsman	£9.95
Colette Bryce	The M Pages	Picador	£10.99
Anne Casey	Out of emptied cups	Salmon Publishing	£10.00
Sarah Cave	Perseverance Valley	Knives Forks Spoons	£16.00
Emily Critchley	alphabet poem: for kids!	Prototype	£12.00
Claire Crowther	Solar Cruise	Shearsman	£9.95
Rishi Dastidar	Saffron Jack	Nine Arches Press	£10.99
Irving Feldman	Usable Truths	Waywiser	£14.99
Peter Finch	The Machineries of Joy	Seren	£9.99
Carolyn Forché	In the Lateness of the World	Bloodaxe Books	£10.99
Matthew Francis	Wing	Faber & Faber	£14.99
Peter Gizzi	Sky Burial: New and Selected Poems	Carcanet	£14.99
Mina Gorji	Art of Escape	Carcanet	£9.99
Philip Gross	Between the Islands	Bloodaxe Books	£10.99
Will Harris	RENDANG	Granta	£10.99
Lesley Harrison	Disappearance	Shearsman	£9.95
David Harsent	Loss	Faber & Faber	£14.99
Michael Haslam	Ickerbrow Trig	Shearsman	£10.95
Jane Hirshfield	Ledger	Bloodaxe Books	£10.99
Katherine Hollander	My German Dictionary	Waywiser	£9.99
Vicente Huidobro	Manifestos	Shearsman	£10.95
Evan Jones	Later Emperors	Carcanet	£9.99
Ed. Eileen Jones & Peter Mortimer	The Iron Book of Tree Poems	Iron Press	£9.00
George Jowett	The Gypsy and the Candy Floss Queen	Smokestack Books	£7.99
Róisín Kelly	Mercy	Bloodaxe Books	£9.95
Emma Lee	The Significance of a Dress	Arachne Press	£8.99
Rupert Loydell & Sarah Cave	A Confusion of Marys	Shearsman	£9.95
André Mangeot	Blood Rain	Seren	£9.99
Clare McCotter	Revenant	Salmon Publishing	£10.00
Antony Owen	The Unknown Civilian	Knives Forks Spoons	£18.00
Ruth Padel	Beethoven Variations	Chatto & Windus	£12.00
Don Paterson	Zonal	Faber & Faber	£14.99
Edward Ragg	Exploring Rights	Cinnamon Press	£9.99
Srinivas Rayaprol	Angular Desire: Selected Poems and Prose	Carcanet	£16.99
Peter Robinson & David Inshaw	Bonjour Mr Inshaw	Two Rivers Press	£15.99
Omar Sabbagh	But It Was an Important Failure	Cinnamon Press	£9.99
Lawrence Sail	Guises	Bloodaxe Books	£9.95
Knute Skinner	An Upside Down World	Salmon Publishing	£10.00
Danez Smith	Homie	Chatto & Windus	£10.99
Ruth Stacey	I, Ursula	V. Press	£10.99
Anne Stevenson	Completing the Circle	Bloodaxe Books	£9.95
Michael Stewart	Couples	Valley Press	£7.99
Marvin Thompson	Road Trip	Peepal Tree Press	£9.99
Alexander Tvardovsky	Vasili Tyorkin: a Book about a Soldier	Smokestack Books	£10.99
Molly Vogel	Florilegium	Shearsman	£12.95
Jennifer Wong	Letters Home	Nine Arches Press	£9.99
Luke Wright	The Remains of Logan Dankworth	Penned in the Margins	£9.99